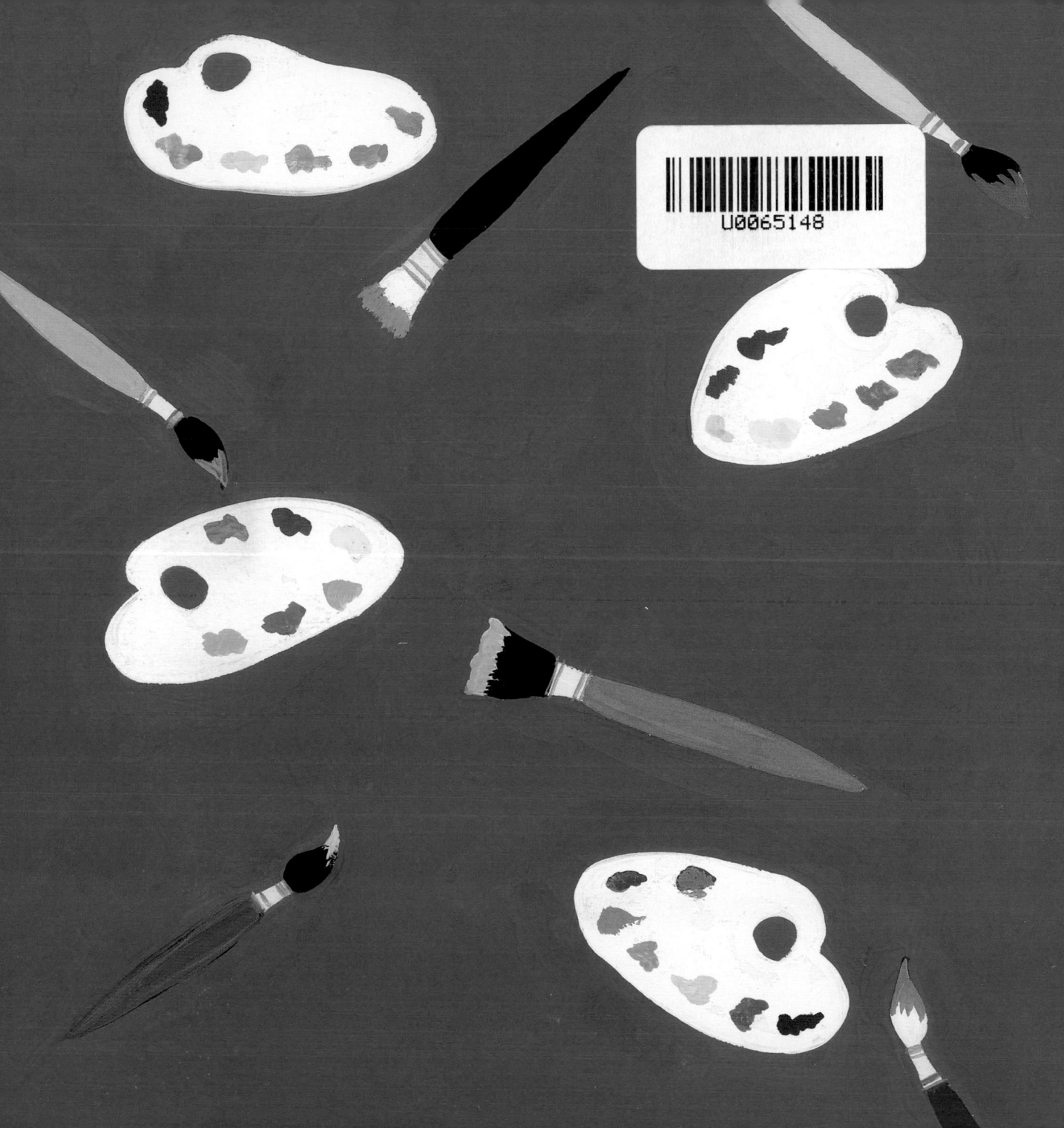

For the students of the
Color Theory class of
Maryland College of Art and Design

Fall 2003 and Spring 2004

Zippy is a clever cat. He can *paint.

He paints pictures of houses.

He paints trees and flowers.

He paints pictures of cats.

Sometimes he paints *mice.

Zippy has a friend named Zoe. Her fifth birthday is on Sunday.

She is having a party with a birthday cake and *balloons.

Zippy wants to make a birthday card for Zoe.

So he gets out his paper.

He gets out his brushes.
He gets out his paints.

He paints the sky blue.

He paints the sun yellow.

He paints some flowers red.

He wants to paint the grass green.

But when he opens the *jar of green paint, it is *empty.

"Oh-oh," says Zippy.

He runs to the store to buy some green paint,
but the store is closed.

14

"Oh no!" cries Zippy.

Zippy feels sad as he walks home. What will he do?
Will he have to paint the grass yellow, red or blue?

Zippy *dips his brush in the blue paint.
*Splat! Some blue falls into the yellow.
"Oops!" says Zippy.

He tries to get the blue paint out of the yellow, but the colors get mixed up. He tries again and they mix some more.

They mix and mix until all the paint turns green.

"Wow!" *shouts Zippy.

Zippy paints the grass green.

He is very excited about making green.

He decides to see what other colors he can make.

He mixes red and yellow together and makes orange.

He mixes red and blue and makes purple.

He mixes red and white and makes pink.

"Cool!" Zippy *exclaims.

So Zippy makes a card for Zoe with all the colors of the rainbow. He gives it to Zoe for her birthday.

Zoe says, "This is the most beautiful card I've ever seen." She *hangs it above the couch. And everyone who sees it loves Zippy's painting.

生字表

adj.= 形容詞 ， n.= 名詞 ， v.= 動詞

賽ㄙㄞˋ皮ㄆㄧˊ與ㄩˇ綠ㄌㄩˋ色ㄙㄜˋ顏ㄧㄢˊ料ㄌㄧㄠˋ

☀ *p.3*

賽ㄙㄞˋ皮ㄆㄧˊ是ㄕˋ一隻ㄓ很ㄏㄣˇ聰ㄘㄨㄥ明ㄇㄧㄥˊ的貓ㄇㄠ，他ㄊㄚ會ㄏㄨㄟˋ畫ㄏㄨㄚˋ畫ㄏㄨㄚˋ。
他ㄊㄚ會ㄏㄨㄟˋ畫ㄏㄨㄚˋ房ㄈㄤˊ子ㄗˇ。

♥ *p.4*

他ㄊㄚ會ㄏㄨㄟˋ畫ㄏㄨㄚˋ樹ㄕㄨˋ和ㄏㄜˊ花ㄏㄨㄚ。
他ㄊㄚ會ㄏㄨㄟˋ畫ㄏㄨㄚˋ貓ㄇㄠ。

☀ *p.5*

有ㄧㄡˇ時ㄕˊ候ㄏㄡˋ，他ㄊㄚ也ㄧㄝˇ會ㄏㄨㄟˋ畫ㄏㄨㄚˋ老ㄌㄠˇ鼠ㄕㄨˇ。

♥ *p.6-7*

賽ㄙㄞˋ皮ㄆㄧˊ有ㄧㄡˇ一個ㄍㄜˋ朋ㄆㄥˊ友ㄧㄡˇ，她ㄊㄚ的名ㄇㄧㄥˊ字ㄗˋ叫ㄐㄧㄠˋ做ㄗㄨㄛˋ柔ㄖㄡˊ依ㄧ。星ㄒㄧㄥ期ㄑㄧ天ㄊㄧㄢ就ㄐㄧㄡˋ是ㄕˋ柔ㄖㄡˊ依ㄧ五ㄨˇ歲ㄙㄨㄟˋ的生ㄕㄥ日ㄖˋ了ㄌㄜ。
她ㄊㄚ會ㄏㄨㄟˋ舉ㄐㄩˇ辦ㄅㄢˋ一個ㄍㄜˋ生ㄕㄥ日ㄖˋ派ㄆㄞˋ對ㄉㄨㄟˋ，派ㄆㄞˋ對ㄉㄨㄟˋ上ㄕㄤˋ會ㄏㄨㄟˋ有ㄧㄡˇ生ㄕㄥ日ㄖˋ蛋ㄉㄢˋ糕ㄍㄠ和ㄏㄜˊ氣ㄑㄧˋ球ㄑㄧㄡˊ。

☀ *p.8*

賽ㄙㄞˋ皮ㄆㄧˊ想ㄒㄧㄤˇ要ㄧㄠˋ做ㄗㄨㄛˋ一張ㄓㄤ生ㄕㄥ日ㄖˋ卡ㄎㄚˇ片ㄆㄧㄢˋ給ㄍㄟˇ柔ㄖㄡˊ依ㄧ，所ㄙㄨㄛˇ以ㄧˇ他ㄊㄚ拿ㄋㄚˊ出ㄔㄨ他ㄊㄚ的ㄉㄜ紙ㄓˇ；

♥ *p.9*

他ㄊㄚ拿ㄋㄚˊ出ㄔㄨ他ㄊㄚ的ㄉㄜ畫ㄏㄨㄚˋ筆ㄅㄧˇ；他ㄊㄚ拿ㄋㄚˊ出ㄔㄨ他ㄊㄚ的ㄉㄜ顏ㄧㄢˊ料ㄌㄧㄠˋ。

p.10

他將天空塗上藍色，

p.11

將太陽塗上黃色，

p.12

還將一些花朵塗上紅色。
他想把草地塗上綠色，

p.13

但是當他打開綠色顏料的罐子時，裡面竟然是空的！
賽皮說：「糟了！」

p.14-15

他跑去商店買綠色的顏料，可是店卻沒有開。
賽皮大叫：「喔，不！」

p.16

賽皮傷心的走回家。他該怎麼辦呢？難道他要將草地塗成黃色、紅色或藍色的嗎？

♥ *p.17*

賽皮拿畫筆沾了沾藍色的顏料。「啪!」的一聲,一些藍色顏料滴進黃色顏料裡了。

賽皮說:「唉唷!」

☀ *p.18*

他試著把藍色顏料從黃色顏料裡弄出來,但這兩種顏色卻混在一起;他又試了一次,結果它們混得更徹底了。

♥ *p.19*

這兩種顏料就這樣不斷的混合,最後全部變成了綠色。

賽皮高興的大喊:「哇!」

☀ *p.20*

於是,賽皮將草地塗上了綠色。能夠製造出綠色來,他覺得好興奮喔!

♥ *p.21*

所以,他決定試試看他還能混合出哪些顏色。

他把紅色跟黃色混合在一起,變成了橘色。

💜 *p.22*

他把紅色跟藍色混合在一起，變成了紫色。

🌻 *p.23*

他把紅色跟白色混合在一起，變成了粉紅色。賽皮驚訝的大喊：「好酷喔！」

💜 *p.24*

後來，賽皮用彩虹的七種顏色畫了一張卡片，送給柔依作為生日禮物。

🌻 *p.25*

柔依說：「這是我看過最漂亮的卡片了！」她把這張卡片掛在沙發上方。每個看到的人都很喜歡賽皮的作品呢！

混色小秘密：

灰色 (grey) = 黑色 (black) + 白色 (white)

咖啡色 (brown) = 紅色 (red) + 綠色 (green)

粉紅色 (pink) = 紅色 (red) + 白色 (white)

淺紫色 (light purple) = 紫色 (purple) + 白色 (white) = 紅色 (red) + 藍色 (blue) + 白色 (white)

色ㄙㄜˋ彩ㄘㄞˇ的ㄉㄜ世ㄕˋ界ㄐㄧㄝˋ

在ㄗㄞˋ「賽ㄙㄞˋ皮ㄆㄧˊ與ㄩˇ綠ㄌㄩˋ色ㄙㄜˋ顏ㄧㄢˊ料ㄌㄧㄠˋ」故ㄍㄨˋ事ㄕˋ中ㄓㄨㄥ，賽ㄙㄞˋ皮ㄆㄧˊ發ㄈㄚ現ㄒㄧㄢˋ原ㄩㄢˊ來ㄌㄞˊ顏ㄧㄢˊ色ㄙㄜˋ是ㄕˋ可ㄎㄜˇ以ㄧˇ被ㄅㄟˋ混ㄏㄨㄣˋ合ㄏㄜˊ出ㄔㄨ來ㄌㄞˊ的ㄉㄜ！下ㄒㄧㄚˋ面ㄇㄧㄢˋ我ㄨㄛˇ們ㄇㄣ就ㄐㄧㄡˋ來ㄌㄞˊ學ㄒㄩㄝˊ習ㄒㄧˊ一ㄧ些ㄒㄧㄝ關ㄍㄨㄢ於ㄩˊ顏ㄧㄢˊ色ㄙㄜˋ的ㄉㄜ事ㄕˋ情ㄑㄧㄥˊ。

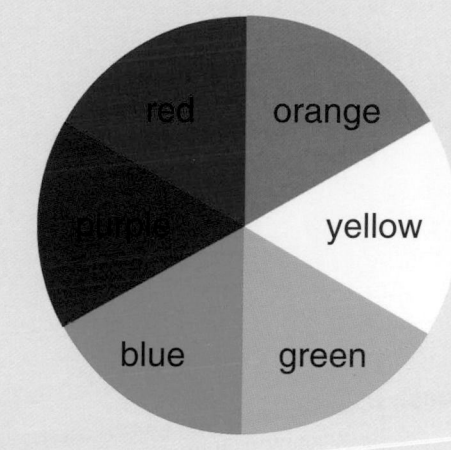

Part. 1 認ㄖㄣˋ識ㄕˋ色ㄙㄜˋ輪ㄌㄨㄣˊ (color wheel)

色ㄙㄜˋ輪ㄌㄨㄣˊ是ㄕˋ由ㄧㄡˊ六ㄌㄧㄡˋ塊ㄎㄨㄞˋ扇ㄕㄢˋ形ㄒㄧㄥˊ組ㄗㄨˇ合ㄏㄜˊ而ㄦˊ成ㄔㄥˊ的ㄉㄜ，表ㄅㄧㄠˇ示ㄕˋ顏ㄧㄢˊ色ㄙㄜˋ跟ㄍㄣ顏ㄧㄢˊ色ㄙㄜˋ之ㄓ間ㄐㄧㄢ的ㄉㄜ關ㄍㄨㄢ係ㄒㄧˋ。

紅ㄏㄨㄥˊ色ㄙㄜˋ、黃ㄏㄨㄤˊ色ㄙㄜˋ、藍ㄌㄢˊ色ㄙㄜˋ被ㄅㄟˋ叫ㄐㄧㄠˋ做ㄗㄨㄛˋ「自ㄗˋ然ㄖㄢˊ界ㄐㄧㄝˋ的ㄉㄜ三ㄙㄢ原ㄩㄢˊ色ㄙㄜˋ」，這ㄓㄜˋ三ㄙㄢ種ㄓㄨㄥˇ顏ㄧㄢˊ色ㄙㄜˋ是ㄕˋ不ㄅㄨˋ能ㄋㄥˊ用ㄩㄥˋ別ㄅㄧㄝˊ的ㄉㄜ顏ㄧㄢˊ色ㄙㄜˋ混ㄏㄨㄣˋ合ㄏㄜˊ出ㄔㄨ來ㄌㄞˊ的ㄉㄜ。

那麼另外三種顏色——橘色、綠色、紫色是怎麼來的呢？仔細觀察下面的圖，再看看色輪，你就會知道答案了！

orange = red + yellow

green = yellow + blue

purple = blue + red

你發現了嗎？在色輪上，橘色、綠色和紫色其實是由相鄰的兩種顏色混合而成的喔！

另外，有兩種沒有出現在色輪上，卻很重要的顏色：黑色和白色。這兩種顏色的作用是調整色彩的明暗度：如果你希望某個顏色可以亮一點，就要加上白色；希望顏色暗一點，就加上黑色。例如：

blue + white = light blue

blue + black = dark blue

Part. 2 小朋友，輪到你來動動腦嘍！猜猜看下面的顏色，各是由什麼顏色混合出來的呢？

（正確答案在第30頁喔！）

grey = _____ + _____

brown = _____ + _____

pink = _____ + _____

light purple = _____ + _____

Author's Note

Writers get ideas for stories from many things. The idea for "Zippy and the Green Paint" comes from my cats and from my students. Zippy and Zoe are my cats. They are best friends. They are very smart and cute.

I teach art to college students. One of the classes I teach is called "Color Theory." The students learn everything about color. They paint color wheels. They learn to mix one hundred colors! The first color they learn to mix is green.

作者的話

作家會從很多東西得到故事的靈感。「賽皮與綠色顏料」這個故事的想法，來自於我的貓和我的學生們。賽皮與柔依是我養的貓，牠們是最要好的朋友，非常聰明可愛。

我在大學教美術，我上的其中一門課叫做「色彩理論」。學生們在這堂課中學習關於顏色的所有事情；他們要畫色輪，還要學會混合出一百種顏色呢！他們第一個學習混合的顏色就是綠色。

About the Author

Carla Golembe is the illustrator of thirteen children's books, five of which she wrote. Carla has won several awards including a New York Times Best Illustrated Picture Book Award. She has also received illustration awards from Parents' Choice and the American Folklore Society. She has twenty-five years of college teaching experience and, for the last thirteen years, has given speaker presentations and workshops to elementary schools. She lives in Southeast Florida, with her husband Joe and her cats Zippy and Zoe.

關於作者

Carla Golembe 擔任過十三本童書的繪者，其中五本是由她寫作的。Carla 曾多次獲獎，包括《紐約時報》最佳圖畫書獎。她也曾獲全美父母首選基金會，以及美國民俗學會的插畫獎項。她有二十五年的大學教學經驗，而在過去的十三年中，曾經在多所小學中演講及舉辦研討會。她目前和丈夫 Joe 以及她的貓──賽皮與柔依，住在美國佛羅里達州東南部。

賽皮與柔依系列

ZIPPY AND ZOE SERIES

想知道我們發生了什麼驚奇又爆笑的事嗎？
歡迎學習英文0-2年的小朋友一起來分享我們的故事 ——
「賽皮與柔依系列」，讓你在一連串有趣的事情中學英文！

精裝／附中英雙語朗讀CD／全套六本

Carla Golembe 著／繪

本局編輯部 譯

Hello！我是賽皮，我喜歡畫畫、做餅乾，還有跟柔依一起去海邊玩。偷偷告訴你們一個秘密：我在馬戲團表演過喔！

Hi，我是柔依，今年最開心的事，就是賽皮送我一張他親手畫的生日卡片！賽皮是我最要好的朋友，他很聰明也很可愛，我們兩個常常一起出去玩！

賽皮與柔依系列有：

1 賽皮與綠色顏料
(Zippy and the Green Paint)

2 賽皮與馬戲團
(Zippy and the Circus)

3 賽皮與超級大餅乾
(Zippy and the Very Big Cookie)

4 賽皮做運動
(Zippy Chooses a Sport)

5 賽皮學認字
(Zippy Reads)

6 賽皮與柔依去海邊
(Zippy and Zoe Go to the Beach)

國家圖書館出版品預行編目資料

Zippy and the Green Paint:賽皮與綠色顏料 / Carla
Golembe 著;Carla Golembe 繪;本局編輯部譯. －
－初版一刷. －－臺北市：三民，2006
　　面；　　公分. －－(Fun心讀雙語叢書.賽皮與柔
　　依系列)
中英對照
ISBN 957–14–4450–2　　(精裝)

　1.英國語言－讀本

523.38　　　　　　　　　　　　　　　94026564

網路書店位址　http://www.sanmin.com.tw

© 　Zippy and the Green Paint
　　　　——賽皮與綠色顏料

著作人	Carla Golembe
繪　書	Carla Golembe
譯　書	本局編輯部
發行人	劉振強
著作財產權人	三民書局股份有限公司 臺北市復興北路386號
發行所	三民書局股份有限公司 地址／臺北市復興北路386號 電話／(02)25006600 郵撥／0009998–5
印刷所	三民書局股份有限公司
門市部	復北店／臺北市復興北路386號 重南店／臺北市重慶南路一段61號

初版一刷　2006年1月
編　　號　S 806171
定　　價　新臺幣壹佰捌拾元整
行政院新聞局登記證局版臺業字第○二○○號

有著作權 · 不准侵害

ISBN　957–14–4450–2　　(精裝)

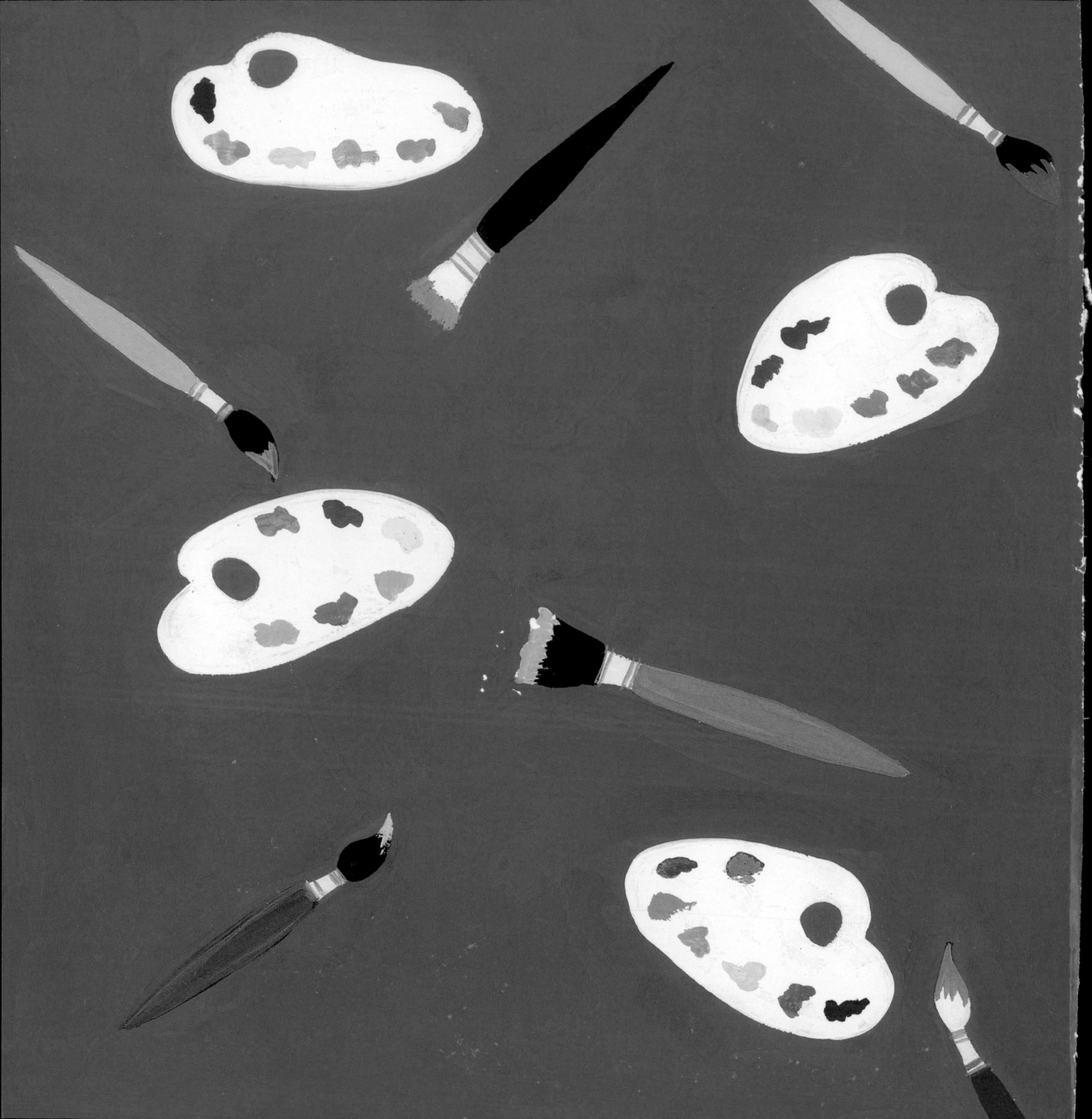